Town Hall Meetings and the
Death of Deliberation

Forerunners: Ideas First

Short books of thought-in-process scholarship, where intense analysis, questioning, and speculation take the lead

FROM THE UNIVERSITY OF MINNESOTA PRESS

(Continued on page 78)

Town Hall Meetings and the Death of Deliberation

Jonathan Beecher Field

University of Minnesota Press

MINNEAPOLIS

LONDON

Published by the University of Minnesota Press, 2019
111 Third Avenue South, Suite 290
Minneapolis, MN 55401–2520
http://www.upress.umn.edu

Available as a Manifold edition at manifold.umn.edu

The University of Minnesota is an equal-opportunity educator and employer.

Contents

Introduction: This Is What Looks like Democracy

ONE OF THE RECURRING THEMES of the first two years of the Trump presidency has been the erosion of democratic norms. The 2018 midterm election witnessed widespread voter suppression in Georgia, alleged vote theft in North Carolina, and a wholesale effort by a lame duck state legislature in Wisconsin to subvert the electoral outcome in the gubernatorial race. These departures from established democratic practices occurred against the background of reckless statements from a president whose blithe disregard for the separation of powers outlined in the U.S. Constitution would be comical if it were not terrifying. Many of these reckless statements reflected the president's concern over ongoing investigations into the possibility that his 2016 electoral victory was in part the result of foreign interference.

This essay is not concerned with these transgressions against the operations of democracy but rather with an ongoing phenomenon that reflects and sustains the conditions that make these transgressions possible. The town meeting is an iconic form of direct citizen democracy. It is increasingly overshadowed by the town hall meeting, however, where those in power unilaterally convey information to their employees or other constituents. Over the past decade or more, the town hall meeting has become a staple of corporate and academic governance. The forms of these town hall meetings are varied, but they all involve announcements and questions about a foregone conclusion, rather than the propositions, deliberations, and votes of an actual town meeting. I do not wish to claim that U.S. citizens cannot tell the difference between a gathering of citizens voting "yea" or "nay" on road improvements in their town versus a CEO of a corporate behemoth holding a press event to unveil a new smartphone. Rather, it does not seem we care much about the difference.

Town Hall Meetings and the Death of Deliberation outlines the town meeting in its original context: as a form of democratic community governance in New England. The essay then traces the structure of the town meeting as it mutates into a format for presidential debates, becomes a staple of corporate governance, and emerges as a way for universities to simulate affective labor. In its most recent iterations, the town hall meeting returns to its local and political roots—but this time with corporate underwriters.

Generations of observers have celebrated the local, direct, and immediate nature of the town meeting as a particularly American form of democracy. This reverence takes an iconic form in artist Norman Rockwell's Four Freedoms series, where the painting Freedom of Speech depicts a man standing up and speaking at a town meeting. The town hall meeting, however, has since emerged as a spectacle designed to emulate the scale and intimacy of the town meeting but lacking direct political consequences. Beginning in the 1992 presidential campaign, the town hall meeting debate format has emerged as a recurring feature of the presidential debate schedule. As opposed to a traditional debate, where the candidates engage with one another directly or respond to questions from a moderator, the town hall format features questions from members of an audience. These debates can have an impact on public opinion, and in turn on voting preferences, but they do not carry the immediate electoral stakes of a town meeting. As Donald Robinson points out in his study of town meetings, the critical feature of the town meeting is that the assembled people discuss and then vote on questions over which they have jurisdiction.[1] Participants in the audience of a town hall–style debate have an indirect influence on the outcome of the election through the questions they pose to the candidates. But the power to decide the election does not lie with the people in the room for the town hall–style debate. The salient difference between a town meeting and a town hall meeting is the devolution from direct jurisdiction to vague influence. Participants in a town hall meeting are in the room where it doesn't happen.

A public gathering that mimics a deliberative democratic process but does not offer any direct power to the people assembled has proved compelling to leaders of various stripes. Especially in the wake of the 2016 election, many elected officials have held town hall meetings to allow constituents to sound off but without directly affecting legislation. Beyond the realm of electoral politics, the town hall meeting has also emerged as a way for college presidents and even CEOs to conduct what amounts to press conferences but with the flavor of democratic ritual.[2] In particular, the political turmoil that attended the presidential campaign and election of Donald Trump resulted in a renewed interest in various forms of social engagement. Many incumbent politicians held town hall meetings that essentially just gave their constituents an opportunity to yell at them. At the same

1. Donald Robinson, *Town Meeting: Practicing Democracy in Rural New England* (Amherst: University of Massachusetts Press, 2011), 2.
2. See https://evp.nd.edu/town-hall/ and https://9to5mac.com/2016/02/04/tim-cook-india-iphone-apple-watch-android/

time, gatherings convened by academic and corporate leaders to unilaterally disseminate information also carry the name of "town hall meeting." These gatherings seem democratic but are ultimately ineffectual.

This essay is thus concerned with the differences between the town meeting and the town hall meeting (sometimes just called "town hall"). These terms sound almost identical and are often confused. In my research for this project, I encountered scholars of deliberative democracy who insisted the terms were fundamentally interchangeable. Indeed, the terms are used in a variety of conflicting ways. For our purposes here, "town meeting" will refer specifically to gatherings open to all citizens of a town. This assembled body of citizens has the power to vote in its elected officials, vote on how to be taxed, and vote on how best to spend the town's money. Put another way, the town meeting is a deliberative assembly that has jurisdictional power over state functions that devolve to local government, most notably the power to tax and to enforce those taxes through the threat of confiscating property or incarcerating a citizen. Conversely this essay will use the phrase "town hall meeting" to refer to assemblies, either public or private, that identify themselves as "town halls" or "town hall meetings." These town hall meetings emulate the direct democratic atmosphere of the town meeting, but the people in attendance do not have any immediate jurisdictional power over the subjects under discussion. For lack of a more elegant term, we can refer to what happens in town meetings as direct democratic deliberative discourse. "Town meeting" and "town hall" are frequently conflated or confused, but the difference is between a structure where citizens have power and one where citizens are either customers or employees.

I come to this topic as a scholar of seventeenth-century New England, and scholars working in this field have a complicated relationship with declension narratives. As L. D. Burnett once observed, "Narratives of declension ain't what they used to be."[3] The argument of Town Hall Meetings and the Death of Deliberation is a declension narrative, because I believe direct democratic deliberation has more to offer U.S. citizens than, say, developers holding a town hall meeting where they listen to complaints they are free to ignore. At the same time, nostalgia for the town meeting can manifest as nostalgia for a whiter and more rural America—where "true democracy" once flourished among hardy souls tucked away in small New England towns—while now all we have is a "vulgar spectacle." Even as we can be sure we are currently confronting all sorts of vulgar spectacles, the argument I still hope to advance is as much an appropriation and proliferation narrative as a declension narrative.

Rather than valorizing the good old days of direct democracy and seeing the present as some sort of perversion of that ideal, I am interested in how the traditional democratic institution of the town meeting has been repurposed in the service of various neoliberal institutions, in particular the university and the corporation. If we consider the transition from seeing people as citizens to seeing people as customers or employees to be a hallmark of neoliberalism, the town hall meeting is an institution that helps manage this transition as smoothly as possible.

Anyone who considers the intersection of democracy and neoliberalism in the contemporary United States writes in the wake of Wendy Brown's work, especially *Undoing the Demos*. In some contexts, "neoliberal" has become a label so freely applied that it can mean not much more than "bad." But for this project, I deploy the term with an understanding that it refers to an ideology of unswerving loyalty to the logic of the market. As

3. L.D. Burnett, "Selling (Out) the Good Old Days," *Society for U.S. Intellectual History* (blog), May 10, 2015, https://s-usih.org/2015/05/selling-out-the-good-old-days/.

Brown describes her argument, "Neoliberalism, a peculiar form of reason that configures all aspects of existence in economic terms, is quietly undoing basic elements of democracy. These elements include vocabularies . . . habits of citizenship . . . and above all, democratic imaginaries."[4] These negative impacts of neoliberalism on democracy point to another uncomfortable question: Are democracy and free markets compatible? For some, of course, democracy and free markets are nearly synonymous—when the U.S. engages in a project to "spread democracy," this effort comes with a promise that free markets are coming right behind democracy, or perhaps even before. At the same time though, it appears that democracy and the free market have a rather uneasy relationship as they exist under late capitalism. Evidence to support this concern is not hard to locate. As Brown details in *Undoing the Demos,* the democracy that the United States brought to Iraq very quickly emerged as one more concerned with free markets than with free people. More specifically, Brown's trope of a "hollowing out" of democracy that she invokes in *Undoing the Demos* resonates with the transformation we see in the town hall meeting. In its later permutations, the form of the town hall meeting remains intact, like the skin of an avocado; but the substance—where all the nutrients are—has been removed, reserved for another time and place.

This transformation may offer a way to think about democracy as having both a form and a substance that can exist independently of each other. The substance of democracy without its form is hard to imagine, and it seems hard to scale beyond an organization of small size. But the form of democracy without its substance is all around us. We see a common example of this when critics assert that institutions do or do not "listen to"

---

4. Wendy Brown, *Undoing the Demos: Neoliberalism's Stealth Revolution.* (Cambridge: Zone/Near Futures, 2015), 17.

people. In a democracy, the most immediate form of being heard is through voting—constituents vote and the incumbent either keeps the job or relinquishes it to a challenger. But for every instance of a contested election, there are dozens of moments when citizens express a grievance or concern. In the wake of a satisfying electoral outcome, it is commonplace to comment that "the people have spoken." This is not the only time people, or the people, speak. But in these other instances, it is harder to discern just who is listening to the people, and what, if anything, they might do in response. As such, one critical aspect of the town hall meeting is something we might call the performance of listening. It is when congresspeople return to their home districts to hold gatherings where constituents can air grievances. The impact of these conversations on future congressional votes, however, can be hard to discern. The performance of politicians in these town hall meetings can have an impact on the overall perception of a candidate and on their chances of reelection. But there is no immediate way that the attendees at one of these meetings hold the political fate of the hosting politician in the same way they would at a town meeting.

To complicate things, listening is a passive act, and it is difficult to see if someone is truly listening. In interpersonal communication, the phrase "I hear you" can be either a genuine expression or an infuriatingly dismissive platitude. Sometimes it can be hard to tell the difference. As we will see, the town hall meeting permits elected officials, university leaders, and CEOs to perform the act of listening in order to mollify a public, especially in situations where that public has no power to give their grievances electoral or budgetary teeth. By stripping it of its deliberative function, the town hall meeting reimagines democracy as something akin to customer service. Unfortunately, the model of customer service is even harder to scale than the deliberative town meeting itself. As Danny Meyer describes it, one of the keys of great customer service is fixing mistakes by overdelivering, or "writing a great last chapter," as he puts it.[5] Your soup was cold? We will take it off the bill, and dessert is on us. Your infrastructure is crumbling? That's harder to fix. Making it right is a viable way to manage individual grievances, because it is one thing to use an institution's resources to soothe a disgruntled customer. But it is untenable if, instead of a customer, you have a public facing the challenges posed by limited resources. Free desserts can fix cold soup, but all the pie in the world won't fix the impact of a bridge closure that adds an hour to your commute.

If Brown is correct in her diagnosis of the current political moment, this essay goes on to detail a set of symptoms visible in the ever-expanding permutations of the town hall meeting as they drift further and further from direct deliberative democracy. This adaptive radiation of democratically conceived public culture into non-democratic forms ultimately works to silence and disenfranchise citizens in a variety of contexts.

There is perhaps some irony in describing the town meeting—a political ritual available to a small minority of (overwhelmingly white and property-owning) U.S. citizens—as democratic, while characterizing the town hall meeting—available in one form or another to most U.S. citizens—as a perversion of democracy. As one indicator of the makeup of many town meetings in New England, the cover of the 2005 book *All Those in Favor: Rediscovering the Secrets of Town Meeting and Community* features small photographs of eighteen different people. They are heterogeneous in terms of age and gender, but all appear to be white.[6]

5. Danny Meyer, *Setting the Table: The Transforming Power of Hospitality in Business* (New York: Harper, 2006), 222.
6. Susan Clark and Frank Bryan, *All Those in Favor: Rediscovering*

True enough, the town hall meeting is "more democratic" in the sense that we might describe a lower-priced version of a luxury good as a more democratic offering. Describing the offerings at the three-star French restaurant Coucou in 2016, Pete Wells observed, "The wine list covers the historic old appellations of France, but it also embraces emerging ones and exciting regions from other countries while pricing bottles in a range that's unusually democratic."[7] In a similar vein, David Landsel proclaimed in *Food & Wine* that, "In-N-Out is perhaps one of the most democratic institutions ever to grace this great democracy. Like everywhere, In-N-Out's prices have been creeping upward in recent years, but the fact remains that there are almost no barriers to enjoying a burger at In-N-Out—a perfectly cooked hamburger, piled high with fresh vegetables and slathered judiciously with tasty spread, still costs just $2.25."[8]

This sense of "democratic" as a synonym for "affordable" is benign on some levels—tasty and affordable food is a good thing, as Martha Stewart might say. At the same time, the conflation also works to erase the distinction between voter and consumer. This use of democratic to mean "economically accessible" recapitulates the neoliberal valorization of the logic of the marketplace as the only logic that matters. As Brown details, "As each term is relocated to the economy and recast in an economic idiom, inclusion inverts into competition . . . freedom into deregulated

the Secrets of Town Meeting and Community (Montpelier: RavenMark, 2005).

7. Pete Wells, "Top New York Restaurants of 2016," *New York Times,* December 13, 2016, https://www.nytimes.com/2016/12/13/dining/best-restaurants-in-nyc-pete-wells.html.

8. David Landsel, "Here's Why It's Time to Stop Comparing In-N-Out to Shake Shack," *Food & Wine, last modified January 24, 2018, accessed January 24, 2019,* https://www.foodandwine.com/news/heres-why-its-time-stop-comparing-in-n-out-shake-shack.

marketplaces, and popular sovereignty is nowhere to be found."[9] And as Lisa Duggan observed along similar lines, "The primary strategy of turn-of-the-century neoliberalism is *privatization,* the term that describes the transfer of wealth *and decision-making,* from public, more-or-less accountable decision-making bodies to individuals or corporate, unaccountable hands."[10]

Tracing the evolution of the town meeting from a deliberative political exercise to a form of electoral theater to an institutional ritual of compassion to a corporate product launch ritual does not mean that subsequent forms replace preceding forms of the town (hall) meeting. Instead, the mutations and permutations continue to exist simultaneously, which makes unraveling their different forms more complicated and more urgent. Chapter 1 offers a description of the town meeting as it functions as a form of direct deliberative democracy, and it considers some of the aspects that have contributed to the mythology of the town meeting as a cornerstone of American democracy. Chapter 2 traces the emergence of the town hall meeting as a format for presidential electoral debates and televised spectacle. Chapter 3 considers how politicians who have been elected use the town hall meeting as a form of constituent service and as a way to perform the act of listening as a form of spectacle in itself. Chapter 4 takes up a similar phenomenon in a different context by investigating the campus town hall as a way for an institution to simulate the process of affective labor. The campus town hall can take different forms: (1) the reactive town hall is held in response to campus trauma, which calls for a performance of institutional affective

9. Brown, 42.
10. Lisa Duggan, *The Twilight of Equality? Neoliberalism, Cultural Politics, and the Attack on Democracy* (Boston: Beacon Press, 2003), 12.

labor; and (2) the informational town hall is where campus leadership announces a new budget or new austerities, and it relies on this form to give the meeting a flavor of democracy, if not its substance. This iteration of the town hall as an entity that unilaterally transfers information is the focus of chapter 5, which takes up the corporate town hall. It can function as a glorified press conference for the public or as a way to deliver bad news to employees in a way that feels somehow more democratic because of the Q&A after the announcement from leadership. Chapter 6 concludes this brief study by considering the ever-expanding universe of town halls, hosted by entities as disparate as Luther Campbell, Bernie Sanders, CNN, Jimmy Buffet, Whole Foods, the Koch brothers, and Fox News.

Town Meeting as Democratic Ideal

A TOWN MEETING is an annual assembly where the citizens of that town elect officials, vote on a budget for the upcoming year, and take up any other matters that may come before the town. Details may vary from town to town and state to state, but typically a minimum of thirty days before the town meeting, town officials announce the date, time, and location of the meeting as well as the issues that will be addressed. Participation and voting are open to all residents of the town who are legal voters. A moderator is elected to run the town meeting, and the usual business consists of hearing and approving reports from various town officials, electing or reelecting new officials, and approving a budget.

This description makes the work of the town meeting sound prosaic and routine. This is a reasonable conclusion to draw. Sometimes there are divisive issues and heated debate, but a town meeting functions very much like any other deliberative body. The work of the town meeting is important on a local level but rarely exciting. What has made the town meeting compelling to generations of observers comes not in the work it does but in who does the work. Virtually every other deliberative body uses elected representatives selected by voters, but the town meeting is a legislative body open to any legal voter within the jurisdiction. At a town meeting, each citizen represents him or herself, and thus the town meeting functions as direct democracy. The town meeting does away with the abstractions inherent in almost any other form of democracy.

In states that employ town meetings, investment in the notion of the town meeting as an ideal form of democracy runs deep. The Vermont secretary of state's website contains a variety of resources to help towns run their meetings. It includes the following greeting: "Town meeting happens every year on the first Tuesday in March. A form of government that exists nowhere else in the world outside of New England, town meeting involves direct citizen lawmaking—true government by the governed. We should feel lucky to live in a place with this unique kind of local government, and community, and we should all do our best to take part."[1] As the secretary of state's comment points out, one of the peculiarities of the town meeting is that it is a form of government almost entirely limited to smaller communities in New England.

Even so, this notion that the town meeting as a form of government is somehow truer than other forms is present in this state official's welcome as well as in scholarship on the town meeting. Frank Bryan's 2010 monograph on the New England town meeting is called "Real Democracy." Bryan writes as a political scientist but also reveals a significant personal investment in the New England town meeting. Bryan's introduction offers a chorus of voices praising this political form, from Timothy Dwight to Alexis de Tocqueville to Ralph Waldo Emerson to Charles Kuralt.

1. The website of the Vermont secretary of state, "Town Meeting and Local Elections," last modified January 9, 2019, https://www.sec.state.vt.us/elections/town-meeting-local-elections.aspx.

And the inclusion of Aleksandr Solzhenitsyn, who spent his exile from the Soviet Union in the small Vermont town of Cavendish, gives a sense of both the range and the limits of the observers who have recorded their regard for the town meeting as practiced in America.[2] In her account of the town meeting ideal and its impact on the nineteenth-century novelist and lawyer Albion Tourgée, Sandra Gustafson describes a character's observation in *Bricks Without Straw,* one of Tourgée's Reconstruction novels: "The presence and absence of the town-meeting . . . in the North and the South constituted a difference not less vital than that of slavery itself."[3] Gustafson points out that John Dewey also deemed the New England style of town meeting a fundamental component of U.S. democracy.

Among these august comments about the town meeting, Tocqueville's observations carry the extra weight of appearing in a classic book on the subject of democracy itself. In this context, it is worth pausing to recall that before democracy was something the United States embraced to the degree that it now occasionally feels obliged to "spread democracy" by force to other nations, democracy was an ideal many leaders regarded with a great deal more ambivalence. The 1669 Fundamental Constitutions of Carolina drafted by John Locke states "that we may avoid a numerous democracy" as one of its reasons for existing.[4] In his less well-known response to Abigail Adams's famous

2. Frank Bryan, *Real Democracy: The New England Town Meeting and How it Works* (Chicago: University of Chicago Press, 2004), 1–28.

3. Sandra M. Gustafson, "Democracy and Discussion: Albion Tourgée on Race and the Town Meeting Ideal," *J19: The Journal of Nineteenth-Century Americanists* 5, no. 2 (2017): 389–96,. https://muse.jhu.edu/ (accessed January 11, 2019), 391.

4. John Locke, "Fundamental Constitutions of Carolina" (*The Avalon Project,* Yale Law School), accessed January 22, 2019, http://avalon.law.yale.edu/17th_century/nc05.asp.

"Remember the Ladies" letter, John Adams responds, "As to your extraordinary Code of Laws, I cannot but laugh. We have been told that our Struggle has loosened the bands of Government every where . . . I begin to think the Ministry as deep as they are wicked. After stirring up Tories, Landjobbers, Trimmers, Bigots, Canadians, Indians, Negroes, Hanoverians, Hessians, Russians, Irish Roman Catholicks, Scotch Renegadoes, at last they have stimulated the[m] to demand new Priviledges and threaten to rebell."[5] Adams's response blends affectionate whimsy with entrenched misogyny, but in his concern about a surplus of democracy, he expresses anxiety that any number of people groups unlike himself are demanding the privilege of self-representation.

Adams's response does suggest one of the persistent limitations of the town meeting as an idealized political form—it has flourished in places that are both rural and overwhelmingly white. In his 1940 celebration of the town meeting, John Gould could write, "Probably the greatest hindrance in New England to continued success with Town Meeting is the influx of strangers—which works in two ways. Many mill towns have received outlanders who speak different languages—and whose nationality and make-up is immediately at odds with Town Meeting traditions. French-Canadians, for example, are fine people—but in politics they organize almost solidly. Organization and Town Meeting are, politically, North and South."[6]

Immediate and direct democracy is untenable in governmental units above a certain small size, and many New England towns

5. John Adams to Abigail Adams, April 14, 1776 The Massachusetts Historical Society, accessed January 22 2019, https://www.masshist.org/digitaladams/archive/doc?id=L17760414ja.
6. John Gould, *New England Town Meeting, Safeguard of Democracy* (Brattleboro, Vt.: Stephen Daye Press, 1940).

have literally outgrown the town meeting. Given the kind of population densities present where a town meeting is a workable form of government, landownership is almost a de facto prerequisite for participating in a town meeting. It is complex to answer how and why the town meeting took hold in the northeast but was not something New England emigrants often brought with them to new settlements as a form of government. But its roots are in the disparate models of settler colonialism deployed in different colonies and extending to the vagaries of internal U.S. migration. Indeed, there is some irony that the aesthetics of the town meeting have been appropriated in so many contexts, while the town meeting itself is a political institution that does not seem to travel well outside of rural New England.

Tocqueville was fascinated by the town meeting as he encountered it in the United States and was surprised not to find it further disseminated. It might be overstating the case to say that it took a French aristocrat to give American democracy a good name, but Tocqueville's *Democracy in America* does serve as a useful monument for U.S. writers who want to celebrate the United States and its institutions. As subsequent observers have pointed out, Tocqueville does make a point of celebrating the town, and particularly the town meeting, as constituted in New England. Tocqueville details at some length why he begins his survey of U.S. government institutions at the local, rather than national, level: "It is not without intention that I begin this subject with the township. The village or township is the only association which is so perfectly natural that, wherever a number of men are collected, it seems to constitute itself." [7]

The larger arc of Tocqueville's project in *Democracy in America*

---

7. Alexis de Tocqueville, *Democracy in America*. University of Virginia American Studies Program, vol. 1, ch. 5. http://xroads.virginia.edu/~hyper/detoc/1_ch05.htm.

is beyond our scope, but he does identify the town as its essential unit. In particular, he explains, "municipal institutions constitute the strength of free nations. Town meetings are to liberty what primary schools are to science; they bring it within the people's reach, they teach men how to use and how to enjoy it. A nation may establish a free government, but without municipal institutions it cannot have the spirit of liberty." For Tocqueville, the very act of participating in a town meeting teaches Americans how to be citizens of a democracy. Given the esteem that many generations of observers have held for Tocqueville, his valorization of the town meeting fulfills itself, to an extent. He does focus on the direct nature of the proceedings as crucial: "In New England the majority act by representatives in conducting the general business of the state. It is necessary that it should be so. But in the townships, where the legislative and administrative action of the government is nearer to the governed, the system of representation is not adopted. There is no municipal council; but the body of voters, after having chosen its magistrates, directs them in." Tocqueville concludes his survey of New England town government with:

> The native of New England is attached to his township because it is independent and free: his co-operation in its affairs ensures his attachment to its interests, the well-being it affords him secures his affection; and its welfare is the aim of his ambition and of his future exertions. He takes a part in every occurrence in the place; he practices the art of government in the small sphere within his reach; he accustoms himself to those forms without which liberty can only advance by revolutions; he imbibes their spirit; he acquires a taste for order, comprehends the balance of powers, and collects clear practical notions on the nature of his duties and the extent of his rights[8]

8. Tocqueville, vol. 1, ch. 5.

For Tocqueville, direct democracy has an almost mystical impact on citizens, as it infuses the "spirit" of democratic forms in their souls.

Considering that Tocqueville construes the town meeting as one of the forces that makes American democracy exceptional, it is not surprising that some of Tocqueville's later readers hold this work in very high esteem. As Harvey Mansfield and Delba Winthrop write in the introduction to their 2000 translation of *Democracy in America,* it is "at once the best book ever written on democracy, and the best book ever written on America . . . If the twentieth century has been an American century, it is because the work of America—not altogether unsuccessful—has been to keep democracy strong where it is alive, and to promote it where it is weak or nonexistent."[9] There are other ways one might choose to characterize the relation of democracy and America in the twentieth century. But this fond recollection of Tocqueville's observations puts the trio of democracy, America, and Tocqueville in a sort of mutual admiration society, and the town meeting emerges as a powerful talisman of this mutual admiration. In Donald Robinson's recent monograph *Town Meeting: Practicing Democracy in Rural New England,* he takes Tocqueville's unfinished business as its warrant: "From his sources in Boston, Tocqueville had gotten the impression that the practices he found in New England had migrated westward, as pioneers from New England moved to the frontier. Alas, by the time he reached Cincinnati a month later, he began to realize that was not true. . . . Now he wished he had studied more carefully the principles, forms, and methods of action" he had

9. Alexis de Tocqueville, *Democracy in America, ed. and trans.* Harvey C. Mansfield and Delba Winthrop (Chicago: University of Chicago Press, 2000), xviii.

found in the towns of New England. That is exactly my goal in the pages that follow.[10]

Robinson is not alone in seeing Tocqueville as a guiding light for American democracy. As Donald Pease details in *The New American Exceptionalism,* Tocqueville becomes something like the brand name for American democracy among certain commentators.[11] In a 1998 piece in *The New Republic* titled "Tocqueville and the Mullah," the journal responded to a CNN interview where Iranian president Mohammad Khatami invoked a number of cherished icons of American political life to suggest that, perhaps, the United States and Iran were not so different. The response of *The New Republic* seems to suggest that the Iranian president should take Tocqueville's name out of his mouth.[12] More generally, though, Pease points out, "From the time of its initial publication in 1835, *Democracy in America* supplied the concepts, generalizations, and categories out of which U.S. citizens were encouraged to experience and make sense of U.S. democracy."[13] (100) As such, Tocqueville's valorization of the town meeting works beyond reasonable expectations as an endorsement that generations of scholars take very seriously.

In the mid-twentieth century, the notion of the town meeting as a fundamental expression of U.S. democracy got a boost from President Franklin Delano Roosevelt and Norman Rockwell. Roosevelt's 1941 State of the Union speech is popularly known as the Four Freedoms speech. Less than a year before the United States would enter World War II following the Japanese attack

10. Donald Robinson, *Town Meeting: Practicing Democracy in Rural New England* (Boston: University of Massachusetts Press, 2011), 5–6.

11. Donald Pease, *The New American Exceptionalism* (Minneapolis: University of Minnesota Press, 2009). 98–128.

12. *New Republic*. "Tocqueville and the Mullah." *February 2, 1998*, 7.

13. Pease, 100.

on Pearl Harbor, Roosevelt confronted the looming threats facing the world and reaffirmed a commitment to four freedoms available to all the citizens of the world. As he detailed:

> In the future days, which we seek to make secure, we look forward to a world founded upon four essential human freedoms. The first is freedom of speech and expression—everywhere in the world. The second is freedom of every person to worship God in his own way—everywhere in the world. The third is freedom from want—which, translated into world terms, means economic understandings, which will secure to every nation a healthy peacetime life for its inhabitants—everywhere in the world. The fourth is freedom from fear—which, translated into world terms, means a world-wide reduction of armaments to such a point and in such a thorough fashion that no nation will be in a position to commit an act of physical aggression against any neighbor—anywhere in the world.[14]

In 1943, the *Saturday Evening Post* commissioned Norman Rockwell to illustrate these freedoms in four paintings, which would then be accompanied by four essays from different authors.[15] *Freedom of Speech* appeared on February 20, 1943, portraying a scene from a New England town meeting and accompanied by an essay by Booth Tarkington. In this painting, Rockwell illustrates Roosevelt's idea of global freedom through a small assemblage of white U.S. citizens. Some Rockwell scholars, however, have observed tension in the painting. The figure standing to speak is wearing clothes that mark him as working class, and he is surrounded by men in suits and ties. It is possible

14. Voices of Democracy, "Franklin D. Roosevelt, 1941 State of the Union Address 'The Four Freedoms Speech,'" January 6, 1941. University of Maryland, Accessed January 23, 2019, http://voicesofdemocracy.umd.edu/fdr-the-four-freedoms-speech-text/.

15. The Norman Rockwell Museum, "Norman Rockwell's Four Freedoms," accessed January 23, 2019, https://www.nrm.org/2012/10/collections-four-freedoms/.

to read the image as another instance of the narcissism of small differences of whiteness, but it does form an iconic image that connects the New England town meeting to a U.S. president's vision of worldwide freedoms. Soon after, these images were enlisted to promote the sale of war bonds.[16] The deployment of the Rockwell posters as part of a national war bond campaign put forth the argument that the New England town meeting represented and embodied the national interest. If World War II was a war to save democracy, then these posters nationalized a very particular form of this democracy to generate financial support for this war. In 1993, the United States Postal Service used images from the Four Freedoms series for a set of four postage stamps. Indeed, the iconic nature of Rockwell's painting has a curiously recursive character. In a 2017 article on the current state of the town meeting in the Vermont alt-weekly *Seven Days,* the lede was: "Town meeting in Kirby resembles an animated version of a Norman Rockwell painting. About 80 residents—of the town's total population of 493—sat side-by-side Tuesday in wooden pews and on metal folding chairs as Republican former state legislator John McClaughry presided over his 51st consecutive Kirby town meeting."[17]

The *Saturday Evening Post* was not the only organ of U.S. conventional wisdom making an ideological investment in the town meeting during World War II. In 1945, *Time* ran a feature titled "Town Meeting Time" that opened like this: "It was fine town-meeting weather. The roads were passable. Spring

16. New Hampshire State Library, "Unifying a Nation: World War II Posters from the New Hampshire State Library," accessed January 23, 2019, https://www.nh.gov/nhsl/ww2/ww04prt.html.

17. Kevin J. Kelley, "Diminishing Democracy? At Kirby Town Meeting, the 18 Percent Rule," *Seven Days,* March 8, 2017, https://www.sevendaysvt.com/vermont/diminishing-democracy-at-kirby-town-meeting-the-18-percent-rule/Content?oid=4488848.

was on its way. The good citizens of New Hampshire met, as they have every spring for 150 years or more, to elect the township officers, approve or amend the budgets, define the general policy of 224 towns for the coming year. It was the purest and the oldest manifestation of democracy in the U.S."[18] In the Cold War era, this national interest of the New England town meeting continued, as *Newsweek* checked in on the recent round of town meetings in the April 4, 1966, issue. In an article titled "New England: Basic Democracy," the magazine shared highlights of deliberations in New London, New Hampshire, and in Harwich and Marblehead, Massachusetts, concluding with a quotation from the Massachusetts assistant attorney general charged with overseeing town meeting law: "The town meeting has endured because it is a very good form of government."[19] *National Geographic* featured scenes from New England town meetings from 1968 in Dresden, Maine, 1974 in Burke, Vermont, and 1992 from the town of Gostnold on Cuttyhunk Island in Massachusetts. The 1974 scene from Vermont is especially compelling. In the original article, an image is captioned, "Under a canvas sky, the Burke town meeting pledges allegiance before getting down to business. In speak-your-mind democracy, all can have their say, and most do."[20]

If these accounts render the persistent ideological and affective investment in the town meeting as a hallmark of American

18. *Time*. "New Hampshire: Town Meeting Tonight." March 26, 1945. Accessed January 23, 2019 http://content.time.com/time/subscriber/article/0,33009,803455,00.html.

19. *Newsweek*. "New England: Basic Democracy." April 4, 1966, 23.

20. Jane Lindholm, Patti Daniels, and Angela Evangie, "Photography Exhibit Remembers a Lost Vermont Era With 'Kodachrome Memory,'" *Here and Now,* Vermont Public Radio, January 22, 2015, http://digital.vpr.net/post/photography-exhibit-remembers -lost-vermont-era-kodachrome-memory#stream/0

democracy in aestheticized form, it is worth clarifying some of the salient features of the town meeting, especially because these are the aspects that tend to vanish as we shift to the town hall meeting. Participants at a town meeting deliberate over questions that that body has jurisdiction over, including which officials to elect, how much to budget for roads, and a host of other local political questions. But the important point is that the power and authority for the decision remain with the people present in the room when the town meeting happens. One useful way to differentiate between a town meeting and town hall meetings in their various forms is to consider the parliamentary structure of a town meeting. A town meeting is a proceeding governed by a form of parliamentary procedure, such as the practices codified in *Robert's Rules of Order*. Parliamentary procedure as a form makes sense for a deliberating body that has jurisdiction as well as the power to tax and spend. At the same time, parliamentary procedure does not make much sense for a town hall meeting, which is either a time for people to air their grievances or a unilateral announcement from an institution to an assembly of people.

The underlying principle of parliamentary procedure is to facilitate a process that respects the rights of both the majority and the minority, ensuring that debate over the matter at hand proceeds in an orderly fashion. The basis of this procedure comes in the form of the motion, where a member of the assembly proposes an action for the assembly to debate. The motion is made and then is either seconded or not. If it is seconded, the motion is up for debate. There is then a period of debate when the chair recognizes members of the assembly who indicate they wish to speak by raising their hands. A member of the assembly can then move to table or call the motion to a vote. If the member has called for the latter, the assembly votes if they wish to vote on the present motion or to continue debate. When the assembly votes to vote on the motion, a voice vote, show of hands, or paper ballot can be used to tally the votes. Not every meeting governed by the rules of parliamentary procedure, more commonly referred to as "Robert's Rules of Order," has full jurisdictional power over every issue it takes up. Faculty meetings, for instance, are usually governed by some form of Robert's Rules, and these bodies often deliberate questions that are ultimately the province of a dean or provost to decide. However, the absence of parliamentary procedure for a so-called town hall meeting does suggest that the body of people assembled does not have jurisdictional power. When, for instance, congresspeople return to their home districts to hold "town hall meetings" with constituents, it is impossible to imagine an incumbent senator taking motions from an audience packed with disgruntled constituents.

When thinking about these various permutations of the town hall meeting, it is helpful to recall the temporality of deliberative rhetoric, which is concerned with things in the future, as opposed to forensic rhetoric, which makes claims about things in the past. A town meeting addresses the future—budget, elections, and maintenance. Conversely, a town hall meeting can be forensic in nature, as leaders of a collegiate or corporate community respond to an event of concern to that population. A corporate or collegiate town hall meeting that addresses things in the future, while articulating a course of action that has already been determined, complicates this taxonomy of the deliberative and forensic. This may explain why these events are popular with political, corporate, and collegiate leaders. Simply by virtue of the name, town hall meetings about things that have happened in the past or have already been decided for the future offer attendees an illusion of deliberative power that they do not, in fact, have.

Alongside the fundamental abstraction of using the language of "town hall meetings," the physical structures of town halls also play a role in the abstraction of a town meeting or town hall meeting. Town meetings usually, but not always, take place in buildings called "town halls." Town hall structures are public buildings that have other uses the 364 days of the year when they are not used for town meetings. The physical space of the town hall can host any number of events: public lectures, AA meetings, Jazzercise classes, auctions for the volunteer fire department, and so on. The pattern of abstraction works something like this: there are public gatherings that happen in town halls that are not town meetings culminating in elections and a budget. These meetings are sometimes called "town hall meetings" for the logical reason that they take place at a town hall. This is a tautology, but any gathering that takes place in a town hall has something of the flavor of a town meeting about it, which helps explain their appeal to campaigning and elected officials. A rally for a presidential candidate is one thing, but a town hall meeting with the same candidate often produces stronger feelings of engagement for attendees. At the next stage of abstraction, gatherings can take place in town halls even though they are not town meetings, just like town halls can be held in spaces that are not physical town halls. Patrick Wolfe famously defines settler colonialism as a structure, not an event. This distinction is useful for thinking about town halls, a phrase that names both structures and events. As such, "town hall" exists in contemporary culture as a signifier that floats untethered from both the structure of the town hall and the function of the town meeting. It can be deployed to name almost any kind of gathering whose organizers want to give an audience the feeling of meaningful participation. Thus, at one end of this series of abstractions, there are moments like, "Escape to Margaritaville mastermind Jimmy Buffett and Hamilton impresario Lin-Manuel Miranda have teamed up for an Escape to Margaritaville town hall conversation that will begin airing today on Sirius/XM."[21] Needless to say, Margaritaville is not a democracy.

Only a fool would attempt to register to vote in the Margaritaville elections. Yet the phrase "town hall conversation" is symptomatic of the work of the town hall meeting, which is to offer conversation in place of a sovereign, deliberative, democratic process that culminates in a vote. Conversation is important, but as John Pat Leary has detailed, "conversation" becomes a way to describe how institutions manage relations with their constituents in a way that divests constituents of power.[22] In what follows, we will trace the various forms these managed conversations can take and consider what impact these burgeoning abstractions of the democratic process might have on democracy itself.

---

21. "Lin-Manuel Miranda and Jimmy Buffett to Discuss Careers on the Radio," *Theatermania*, March 22, 2018, https://www.theatermania .com/broadway/news/lin-manuel-miranda-and-jimmy-buffett-conversation_84552.html.

22. John Patrick Leary, *Keywords: The New Language of Capitalism* (Chicago: Haymarket, 2018), 48–49.

Town Hall Meeting as Debate Format

ONE OF THE FIRST POLITICIANS to grasp the national potential of the New England town hall's physical space was Jimmy Carter. Early in his term, "His aides carefully scouted small towns with historic physical halls and a strong local government in which to launch the president's 'meet the people' tour. In the Irish Catholic town center of Clinton, Massachusetts, in a small but stately yellow brick building, Carter answered questions from a largely Irish Catholic community who packed the floor level up to the balcony."[1] According to the *New York Times,* "White House staff members were jubilant last night over what they considered the public relations triumph of their visit here."[2]

Fifteen years later, Bill Clinton, another southern political candidate, worked even harder to capture the mystique of the

---

1. Molly Osberg, "How Bill Clinton and MTV invented the once-thrilling, now-meaningless town hall debate," *Splinter News,* October 9, 2016, https://splinternews.com/how-bill-clinton-and-mtv-invented-the-once-thrilling-n-1793862627.

2. John Kifner, "Clinton Back to Normal after Carter's visit," *New York Times,* March 18, 1977, 11 https://www.nytimes.com/1977/03/18/archives/clinton-back-to-normal-after-carters-visit.html.

New England town hall for his campaign. As a small state with huge electoral stakes, New Hampshire voters are accustomed to a level of in-person campaigning that is impossible in other states. With some time and energy, it is possible for a New Hampshire voter to meet all of the candidates in a presidential electoral cycle in person. Bill Clinton's campaign popularized calling these meetings "town hall meetings." The 1992 New Hampshire primary campaign overlapped with some of the most challenging moments in Bill Clinton's presidential career. He joined the rest of the primary field in conceding the Iowa caucus to native son Tom Harkin, but he faced a formidable challenge in New Hampshire from Paul Tsongas of neighboring Massachusetts. The New Hampshire primary took place on February 17, 1992, and the first six weeks of that year witnessed allegations of Clinton's infidelity and draft dodging. The famous Bill and Hillary *60 Minutes* appearance happened on January 26 of that year. These allegations took their toll in the polls. Close to primary day, Bill Clinton hosted televised town halls, which took the form of the candidate buying thirty minutes of time on a local TV station and answering questions from a studio audience.

As Mandy Grunwald recalled in 2016: "We all had confidence that if people could just see Bill Clinton and hear him, they'd be for him. It was very hard with the media covering all this junk. So we said, 'Let's create our own shows.' So we bought 30 minutes of television time on Thursday and Friday night [February 13 and 14] and had these televised town halls."[3] In retrospect, Grunwald recalls these events as "televised town halls"; it is not clear how often that name was used for these events. At the time, the *New*

3. Patrick Healy, "Resurrection: How New Hampshire Saved the 1992 Clinton Campaign," *New York Times,* February 8, 2016 (accessed January 23, 2019), https://www.nytimes.com/interactive/2016/02/08/us/politics/bill-hillary-clinton-new-hampshire.html.

York Times, in covering these two appearances, simply refers to them as "30-minute live call-in show[s] that [were] televised during prime time on a Manchester station."[4]

These two televised performances played a role in salvaging Clinton's New Hampshire campaign, which managed a strong second-place finish against local hero Tsongas, a result which Clinton's campaign spun by calling the Arkansan "The Comeback Kid." With this success in mind, the Clinton campaign advanced the idea of a "town hall" format debate during the general election against incumbent President, George H. W. Bush. Between February and October, the name "town hall" became much more firmly attached to this kind of event—the debate was billed explicitly as such, and the commentators made a point of mentioning the uniqueness of this format.

Regular and formal debates between presidential candidates are a relatively recent phenomenon. After the famous Lincoln–Douglas debates of 1856, the practice lapsed for more than a century, until the equally famous Kennedy–Nixon debates took place in 1960. It is conventional wisdom that these latter debates demonstrated the importance of image in politics in the age of television—Kennedy was young and energetic, Nixon was tired and unshaven—but these debates did offer substantive opportunity for the candidates to engage with each other. The format of the first debate allowed each candidate eight minutes to make an opening statement, which is an eternity in contemporary television. The format of presidential debates over the ensuing three decades has generally been this mod-

4. Gwen Ifill, "The 1992 Campaign: New Hampshire; Clinton Stressing His Economic Plan," *New York Times,* February 15, 1992, 1 (accessed January 25, 2019), https://www.nytimes.com/1992/02/15/us/the-1992-campaign-new-hampshire-clinton-stressing-his-economic-plan.html.

el: candidates are on stage with a panel of journalists who ask questions. 1992 saw the first "town hall–style" debate. Instead of journalists, questions came from a panel of undecided voters, who also served as the audience for the debate. The appeal of this format is self-evident, especially if one considers the debates first and foremost as a spectacle. This format purportedly put the power in the hands of the people rather than journalists. But what power, and what people?

The principle difference between a regular debate and a town hall debate is that instead of questions from a panel of journalists, questions come from "real people," specifically undecided voters. In subsequent town hall debates, undecided voters are selected from across the country and flown to the location of the debate, where they constitute the audience. There are all sorts of caveats one could offer about any effort to define "real people." The important thing seems to be that real people exist in contrast to "the media," which in this case, means journalists. For the effect of the town hall meeting format is to remove journalists almost entirely from involvement in the process. Indeed, one of the curious aspects of the town hall debate is that the media organizations that present them perform this ritual of self-erasure.

In place of elite and aloof media hacks, regular people make a town hall meeting a town hall meeting. This language evokes the town meetings discussed in the previous chapter, but the body of people assembled for a town hall debate fills an entirely different function. The people in the room during these debates have no jurisdictional power. They are voters, and undecided voters at that, but they do not cast votes as the result of their deliberations occasioned by their gathering together. Their power exists not in any direct influence they might have on what happens the evening they gather, but in the influence they have on the spectacle that is broadcast to millions of viewers across the nation. At the openings of these debates, there is usually a moment when the host indicates that instead of journalists asking questions, tonight the people are in charge. At the same time, of course, "the people," represented by a studio audience, are conscripted into a media spectacle. Instead of a revolution that puts you in the driver's seat, it is a revolution that hands you the controls for a video game that simulates driving.

The introduction to this 1992 debate suggests that its organizers had high hopes for the format. As moderator, Carole Simpson of ABC emphasized the historic nature of this debate, opening the telecast with:

> My name is Carole Simpson, and I will be the moderator for tonight's ninety-minute debate, which is coming to you from the campus of the University of Richmond in Richmond, Virginia. Now, tonight's program is unlike any other presidential debate in history. We're making history now, and it's pretty exciting. An independent polling firm has selected an audience of 209 uncommitted voters from this area. The candidates will be asked questions by these voters on a topic of their choosing—anything they want to ask about. My job as moderator is to, you know, take care of the questioning, ask questions myself if I think there needs to be continuity and balance, and sometimes I might ask the candidates to respond to what another candidate may have said.[5]

If not as decisive a victory as Kennedy over Nixon in 1960, the form suited Clinton much better than Bush—while the incumbent glanced at his watch, the challenger channeled the work he had put in to rehearsing for this event by hitting his marks on stage and connecting with the audience. This "October moment" gave the Clinton campaign some much-needed momentum and is credited by some observers with propelling the former Arkansas governor to victory in November. With shades

5. "Presidential Debate at the University of Richmond," The American Presidency Project, UC-Santa Barbara (accessed January 25, 2019), https://www.presidency.ucsb.edu/node/217084.

and saxophone solos on *Arsenio,* Bill Clinton earned the sou-briquet of "The MTV President," and performances like these were part of the reason why.[6] There are others who are better qualified to consider if a town hall debate makes for better electoral politics than the more traditional debate format. Indeed, the emphasis that this kind of coverage of electoral politics puts on the undecided voter diminishes attention to the role that factors like turnout and voter suppression have in determining the outcome of elections. My concern is not with the influence that this debate format might have on U.S. electoral politics, but rather how influential this model of a simulacrum of democracy has been for how universities and corporations relate to their constituents.

If the 1992 presidential campaign marked the moment the town meeting and the town hall meeting began to drift apart—with the town hall meeting taking on a life beyond the town hall—it is worth considering what each thing is and is not. Like a town meeting, the town hall meeting debate permits direct engagement between constituents and elected officials. Unlike a town meeting, that engagement does not have a direct or immediate impact on any vote. In a town meeting, everyone present hears a question and its response, and everyone present votes during the course of that same meeting. By contrast, a question in a town hall debate occurs some number of weeks before the election, is heard by a television audience who may or may not be willing or able to vote, and may or may not recall the impact of a particular question. As such, the crucial shift with the advent of the town hall meeting is a decoupling of the performative from the deliberative aspects of democracy. The

6. Jose Antoino Vargas, "Bill Clinton—The MTV President," SFGate. January 21, 2001 (accessed January 25, 2019), https://www.sfgate.com/news/article/Bill-Clinton-The-MTV-President-2961362.php.

participants in a town hall meeting perform the rituals of democracy, but they do not vote. Like faculty at a university commencement, this is an audience that exists to be seen as much as it does to observe. As a body of people, the audience assembled for a town hall resembles the audience for a program like *The Price Is Right* more than it does the citizens who gather for a town meeting—a lucky few will be called to participate, but even their participation is primarily for the benefit of those watching at home on TV.

Since the 1992 town hall presidential debate, the town hall debate in various forms has been a regular part of the presidential debate schedule. One of the curiosities of the 1996 town hall debate are the layers of audience: the constructed town hall on the stage, the audience in the auditorium watching the audience on stage, and then the audience watching on television at home.

The 2016 town hall presidential debate happened right after the release of the notorious video of Donald Trump describing his habit of grabbing women by their genitals. In an effort to change the conversation, among the guests joining Trump's debate contingent were three women who alleged sexual abuse by Secretary Clinton's husband. Many anticipated that the video revelations would be the end of Trump's campaign, but the candidate's deployment of human props representing Bill Clinton's transgressions suggests that Trump's understanding of the the intrinsically theatrical nature of a town hall helped him survive this challenge. Rhetorical performances in the context of a deliberative democracy can be theatrical, but you cannot fly in human props to help support your argument in an actual town meeting. If nothing else, this Trump–Clinton debate suggests the importance of an electorate capable of understanding the difference between deliberation and spectacle.

The context of these revelations and counterattacks also produces a curious conflation of theatrical and deliberative imagery.

As a CBS News commentator observed when introducing the 2016 town hall debate (at 2:47), "This was supposed to be about the voters on the stage, but . . ."

This town hall debate was held on October 9, 2016, and was hosted by Martha Raddatz of ABC and Anderson Cooper of CNN. As Cooper explained, a town hall debate "gives voters the chance to directly ask the candidates questions. Martha and I will ask follow-up questions, but the night really belongs to the people in this room and to the people across the country who have submitted questions online." Cooper explained that the people in the room had been selected by the Gallup organization from undecided voters in the Saint Louis area.

Anderson Cooper opened the debate with, "We will begin the debate with a question from one of the members in our town hall." It is hard to figure out exactly what this town hall was or what it meant to be a "member" of it. Cooper described the physical space as a room on the campus of Washington University that had been converted into a TV studio. The members of this town hall were undecided voters selected by a polling organization. Essentially, ambivalence was a requirement for taking part in this body.

It is understandable that for the sake of the debate's atmosphere, the organizers preferred not to have hardcore partisans of one candidate or the other asking questions. But the format did make something of a fetish of the relatively small number of voters who had not yet made up their minds. Indeed, if the fiction of the town hall debate is that the assembled voters are a representative sample of the electorate at large, the focus on undecided voters privileges a segment of citizens occupying a relatively narrow portion of the political spectrum. It is possible to imagine an alternative, where the television town hall is populated according to current polling: 43 percent for Candidate A, 37 percent for Candidate B, and 20 percent who are undecided.

However, the kind of discourse this format would produce would likely do even more to reinforce extant preferences than the current format. Actual town meetings can and do get contentious, but they tend not to contain the kind of personal attacks that inform so much of contemporary presidential electoral politics. It is, one imagines, possible to persuade voters by informing them at a town meeting: "We need to increase the road budget, because that bridge will fall down if we don't fix it." On the other hand, presidential debates rarely allow voters the opportunity to learn new information about candidates and their stances. A question, then, remains: "Is genuinely deliberative presidential electoral politics even possible?"

If Bill Clinton pioneered the town hall meeting as a political form, his spouse adapted these gestures in her own campaigns. A 2007 CBS news report described the transition to "Hillary 2.0": "When Hillary Clinton began her run for U.S. Senate in 1999, she embarked on a statewide 'listening tour,' for which she trudged through every county of New York State, visiting with small groups and paying particular attention to conservative upstate regions. It worked. Seven years later, Clinton is trying her old routine, but with a cyber twist. In the era of Web 2.0, meet Hillary 2.0." As the article explains, "Instead of rural town hall campaigning, Clinton is meeting voters in online video chats, from the comfort of a living room—or at least a pretty convincing staged couch-and-computer setup—for 'conversations,' in which viewers can type out and submit questions."[7]

An article in the *New York Times* from the same time describes the process in more detail:

7. Christine Lagorio, "Meet Hilary 2.0," CBS News, March 8, 2007 (accessed January 26, 2019), https://www.cbsnews.com/news/meet -hillary-20-24-01-2007/

By the time she was done with her inaugural two-day trip as a presidential hopeful on Sunday evening, it was clear that the candidate who trudged across New York almost seven years ago did not show up in Iowa this weekend. This candidate Clinton did a lot more talking than listening. She offered an assertive case against the Bush administration and for her own qualifications to be president.[8]

The image of Hillary Clinton trudging across every county of New York State on a self-described "listening tour" as a prelude to her first political campaign as a candidate raises some questions about the kind of gendered political reactions all of her candidacies have elicited in various contexts; but there are other scholars who have considered those questions in depth. It is interesting to note that if the relation between talking and listening is one of the salient questions of how town hall meetings work, the gendered norms that surround those two activities are worth considering as part of the framework of any deliberative or faux deliberative situation. A detail from the *New York Times* article is telling: "But for all her effort to restage the 2000 campaign here—'Let the conversation begin!' read the banner at her town hall meeting—this is a very different year and a very different campaign." The town meeting becomes a town hall meeting becomes a conversation. Conversation can be edifying, but it does not carry the force of law. John Pat Leary considers "the conversation" as a totem of contemporary U.S. culture: blogs, news sites, and other media employ the euphemism of "conversation" to refer to any managed interaction with viewers, readers, or listeners. What was once confined to the Letters to the Editor page is now channeled through social media and online comment

8. Adam Nagourney, "Hilary takes a New Tack, and Talks," *The New York Times,* January 28, 2007, p, A14 (accessed January 26, 2019), https://www.nytimes.com/2007/01/29/us/politics/29clinton.html.

threads that simulate a casual exchange between peers—what most people would call a "conversation."[9]

However, as Leary details, "Taken literally, therefore, a conversation has almost nothing in common with any individual's actual relationship to any bureaucratic institution, much less the modern mass media and advertising industries." "Conversation," however, remains a popular way for politicians to imagine their relation to constituents, as Leary observes. In the United States, "national conversations about race" have been proclaimed, demanded, and denounced at least since Bill Clinton's use of the phrase in his 1997 "Initiative on Race." The limitations of this invocation are significant: "Since a 'national conversation' about anything is a logical impossibility, many, if not most, invocations of the phrase are actually about how the conversation never took place, or never will."[10]

The *New York Times* article about Hillary Clinton campaigning in Iowa reveals this impossible conversation but does not comment on it as such: "An estimated 1,000 people turned out to see her at the town hall event on Sunday morning, prompting organizers to move it from a restaurant to an exhibit hall at the state fairgrounds. Mrs. Clinton spent an hour taking questions and lingered for nearly another hour talking to anyone who could push through the crowd. An intimate chat it was not."[11] Again, there are some presumptions that when a female politician invites voters to a "conversation," it will be an intimate chat. At the same time, a gathering of 1,000 people, all focused on a single

9. John Pat Leary, "The Conversation," *Keywords for the Age of Austerity* (blog), May 22, 2014, https://theageofausterity.wordpress.com/2014/05/22/keywords-for-the-age-of-austerity-6-the/.

10. Leary, "The Conversation."

11. Nagourney, A14

candidate, cannot be a "conversation" in the commonly accepted use of the term.

The contrast between Clinton's senatorial and presidential campaigns throws some of the rhetorical perversity of naming these events "town halls" into sharper relief, but the deployment of the town hall as a campaign strategy is commonplace and bipartisan. The conversation (which is not a conversation) at an event called a town hall (that takes place in a venue that is not a town hall) is par for the course in contemporary U.S. politics across the political spectrum.

Town Hall Meeting as Constituent Service

NOT MANY WEEKS separated the infamous Trump–Clinton town hall–style debate from the "town hall meetings" many elected officials felt compelled to hold in the winter of 2017. These town hall meetings offered something quite different from what town hall–style presidential debates offered viewers. In general, these constituent service town hall meetings do not offer viewers or attendees the sense that they hold the fate of the featured politician in their hands. Instead of an exchange between candidates that viewers can use to inform their voting decisions, the constituent service town hall meeting provides already-elected politicians the opportunity to cement their incumbent status. These constituent service town hall meetings reflect an ongoing shift in political culture, as Greg O. Jones described in an early iteration in 2000: "An instinctive campaigner, Bill Clinton promoted a more public style of governing, a development referred to by some as 'permanent campaigning.'"[1]

1. Charles O. Jones, "Nonstop! The Campaigning Presidency and the 2000 Presidential Campaign," The Brookings Institution, December 1, 2001 (accessed January 26, 2019), https://www.brookings.edu/articles/nonstop-the-campaigning-presidency-and-the-2000-presidential-campaign/.

These meetings can go well or poorly, and the hosting politician can lose their cool or not. But nothing is immediately at stake as there is in the town meeting or even indirectly at stake as there is in the town hall–style debate preceding an election. These meetings, in fact, owe more to the kind of campaign town hall meeting pioneered by Bill Clinton than they do to any kind of deliberative political activity. In spite of this obvious limitation, constituent service town hall meetings are popular, and constituents berate their congresspeople when they fail to hold them. There is an organization that maintains web resources to help interested citizens keep track of when a town hall meeting will take place near them. Town Hall Project's slogan is "Show Up, Speak Out." As they describe their mission, "Town Hall Project empowers constituents across the country to have face-to-face conversations with their elected representatives. . . . We come from a diversity of backgrounds and live across the country. We share progressive values and believe strongly in civic engagement. We research every district and state for public events with members of Congress. Then we share our findings to promote participation in the democratic process."[2]

The work the Town Hall Project does is laudable, but its own account of this work reveals the slippage of the town meeting into the town hall meeting. On their About page, one of the questions is "Why town halls?" and they answer like this: "There is no better way to influence your representatives than in-person conversations. Town halls are a longstanding American tradition—where our elected representatives must listen and respond to the concerns of their constituents. Remember: you are their boss."[3] This statement may fetishize the embodied nature of

2. "About," Town Hall Project (accessed January 26, 2019), https:// townhallproject.com/#about.
3. "About," Town Hall Project (accessed January 26, 2019), https:// townhallproject.com/#about.

democratic politics in a way that is anachronistic in the current media landscape. But it also obscures the differences between a town meeting—which is a longstanding American tradition and where the members have immediate political power—and town hall meetings. Like the gatherings cataloged by the Town Hall Project, town hall meetings will, at best, push public opinion in one direction or another, and they are not a longstanding American tradition (at least not by the name of "town hall").

Town Hall Project's statement of purpose concludes: "We believe every citizen, no matter the party of their members of Congress, should have the opportunity to speak with his or her representatives. You have more power than you think. Town halls are one of the most effective ways to use it." It is difficult to be cynical about this conception of contemporary U.S. politics, but it is important to be clear about what is and is not at stake in these constituent service town hall meetings. By definition, an organization that "empowers constituents across the country to have face-to-face conversations with their elected representatives" is focused on engaging with incumbent politicians who have already been elected to an office. These meetings can be compelling political theater, but the actual political change they can accomplish comes down to two possibilities: (1) a congressperson hears testimonies that move him or her to change positions on a given issue; or (2) the congressperson's performance at these political rituals is so poor that it costs his or her seat in the next election. Given the host of other forces that shape politics—lobbying, television, social media—it is hard to think of an instance when either outcome could be attributable to the voluntary town hall meetings Town Hall Project calls elected officials to have.

In any event, Town Hall Project treats the willingness to hold these meetings as a significant litmus test for politicians. It maintains a Missing Members list on its website: "162 members of Congress have not held a single in-person town hall since January 1, 2017. Is yours one of them?"[4] In a similar vein, Town Hall Project has promoted the #townhallpledge campaign, which asks candidates to pledge that they will hold at least four public meetings a year. It is good to encourage elected officials to be more accessible to their constituents but calling these gatherings "town hall meetings" suggests they are more powerful than they actually are.

To consider a particular example, in the context of the rhetoric of accountability that surrounds the constituent service town hall meeting, the atmosphere of Lindsey Graham's town hall meeting on March 4, 2017, was surprisingly jocular. Senator Graham began with, "Play ball!" and announced that they would be finished in time for everyone to watch the Clemson–Carolina baseball game.[5]

The audience, which was largely anti-Graham, seemed to enjoy the back and forth with their antagonist. But the mood changed a little more than ten minutes in when Graham literally wagged his finger at an attendee who disputed the senator's account of problems with Obamacare, telling him he would "get kicked out if you don't shut up . . . because you're rude." The conversation that unfolded included questions concerning many of the major issues of the moment, including health care, Russian interference in the election, and Supreme Court nominees. Near the end of the event, Graham made a comment that summed up the tenor of the conversation: "People came here

4. Town Hall Project (@townhallproject), "Is your MOC a 'Missing Member?'" Twitter, April 27, 2018, 7:42 p.m., https://twitter .com/townhallproject/status/990013261713059840.

5. Senator Lindsey Graham Town Hall Meeting, C-SPAN, March 4, 2017 (accessed January 26, 2019), https://www.c-span.org/ video/?424917-1/senator-lindsey-graham-town-hall-meeting.

thinking that if you yell at me enough I'll stop being a conservative Republican, and I won't. Some people came here believing that I'll never help Trump because I say bad things about him. I will, but I'm still going to push back when I think he's wrong." Earlier in the meeting, at 45:25, Graham replied to a follow-up question about his support for Betsy DeVos: "We're talking about foreign aid. I've answered the DeVos question. If you don't like it, you don't like it." And earlier, at 44:02, Graham observed, "There are consequences to losing an election." These comments suggest that Senator Graham viewed his 2014 electoral victory as a mandate to pursue what he felt was best for his constituents for the duration of his term, and he communicated as much in this meeting. There were almost 673,000 South Carolinians who voted to reelect Graham in 2014, and there were no more than 1,000 who attended this town hall in 2017. So, it would be unreasonable to expect major changes from Graham as a result of a gathering like this. At the same time, it may be that the principle benefit of a constituent town hall is to provide catharsis for unhappy constituents. At 1:01:35, Graham suggested he understood as much when he said, "A lot of people out here . . . are so upset about Trump. You have no idea what it takes to run a democracy. You're so upset, you're so bitter that you can only see one side of the story." Graham's comments remind us, this is a conversation that happens after an election rather than a conversation that has immediate impact on a vote.

Graham's performance also reminds us that while town meetings are about institutions, town hall meetings are often about personalities. This is "Lindsey Graham's Town Hall" rather than a gathering that involves a political jurisdiction. As attendee Tara Burnett explains at 36:00, Graham held the town hall in response to a petition from a constituent. Unlike an election, State of the Union address, or town meeting, there is no law that compels Senator Graham or his colleagues to hold events like this. A petition underscores the voluntary nature of the meeting:

> Constituents of Tim Scott and Lindsey Graham would like to request a town hall meeting to discuss a variety of issues. . . . A town hall meeting would give you the opportunity to communicate with your constituents in larger numbers, and would grant us the opportunity to clearly understand your positions and to voice our own concerns. We would like to schedule this meeting as soon as possible.
>
> Thank you,
> Residents of South Carolina[6]

Constituents "would like" and close by saying "thank you." Good manners can be a good thing, but the please-and-thank-you dynamic informing this event limits its political efficacy. In contrast, the formal announcement that a town meeting will soon take place is called a "warning." There is a tone of deference here that runs counter to the idea that congresspeople are the employees of their constituents. As we saw in the case of Steven Salaita's dismissal from a tenured position at the University of Illinois, invoking civility can work to derail conversations about things that are more harmful than bad manners. Here, Graham traded on this dynamic when he threatened to kick out a constituent for being "rude," and much of the coverage of the many constituent service town hall meetings held in early 2017 focused on the boisterous nature of the proceedings.

Indeed, "raucous town hall meeting" was a favorite phrase during coverage of these events in the wake of Trump's election. While the *Greenville News* used the phrase to describe Senator

---

6. Senator Tim Scott and Senator Lindsey Graham Town Hall Meeting Request, Change.org (accessed January 27, 2019), https://www.change.org/p/town-hall-meeting-request-for-sc-senator-scott-and-senator-graham.

Graham's town hall meeting in Clemson, Louisiana Senator Bill Cassidy was the first to have his own "raucous town hall meeting" in February 2017. The list of 2017 "raucous town hall meetings" continued: Texas Representative Pete Sessions had one in March; Arizona Senator Jeff Flake had one in April; Maryland Representative Dave Brat had one in May. In one of the more extreme cases, California Representative Tom McClintock left a "raucous town hall meeting" with a police escort.[7]

The persistently raucous nature of these meetings owes something to the political mood in the country following Trump's election; but it might also have something to do with the intrinsically frustrating nature of these meetings. Imagine a subset of constituents who confront a congressperson who has most likely been elected in spite of the votes of those attending the town hall meeting. In this respect, the town hall meeting has a different function than the kind of rallies Donald Trump frequently holds. As attendees at constituent service town hall meetings

7. Paul Hyde, "Senator Graham Gets an Earful in Raucous Town Hall Meeting," *Greenville News,* March 4, 2017, https://www.greenvilleonline.com/story/news/2017/03/04/graham-gets-earful-raucous-town-hall-meeting/98699218/; "Sen. Bill Cassidy Presides over Raucous Town Hall Meeting," Nola.com, February 22, 2017, https://www.youtube.com/watch?v=gAMqsuIMGxY; Gromer Jeffers Jr, "After Confronting Pete Sessions at Raucous Town Hall, Can Democrats 'Vote Him Out' in 2018?," *Dallas News,* March 1, 2017, https://www.dallasnews.com/opinion/commentary/2017/03/22/confrontingpete-sessions-raucous-town-hall-can-democrats-vote-2018; Bryan Logan, "Sen. Jeff Flake Gets Slammed in Raucous Town Hall Meeting," AOL, April 14, 2017, https://www.aol.com/article/news/2017/04/14/republican-sen-jeff-flake-gets-slammed-in-raucous-town-hall-meeting/22039773/; Sarah Rankin, "Dave Brat Hears an Earful," *US News & World Report,* May 9, 2017, https://www.usnews.com/news/best-states/virginia/articles/2017-05-09/virginia-rep-brat-hosts-raucous-town-hall; Angela Hart, "McClintock Exits with Police Escort after Raucous Town Hall Meeting in Roseville," *The Sacramento Bee,* February 6, 2017.

speak, politicians perform the postures of listening, while still reaffirming the views that got them elected in the first place. In the absence of parliamentary rules like the ones that govern a town meeting, the rules that govern a town hall meeting are less distinct but do tend to default to some conception of politeness—or transgressions on politeness, what with all the raucousness these meetings evidently engender. Politeness has its place, but it can be a luxury a democracy cannot afford.

While a town meeting has a moderator, a town hall meeting has a host. A moderator of a town meeting is empowered to keep order, up to having obstreperous attendees removed by police, even as a majority of citizens can overrule the decisions of the moderator. Rather than the standard of order implied by a moderator, a host suggests a different standard of civility. Civility and democracy are not inimical to one another, but they can be uneasy companions. The question of what is or is not "personal" (or polite or civil) overlaps with the putative status of the constituent service town hall meeting as a way to hold elected officials accountable. Guides to parliamentary procedure like *Robert's Rules of Order* point out that personal remarks are not appropriate during deliberation.[8] In the context of a constituent service town hall meeting, the focus of the meeting is the person holding the meeting, so it is difficult for any comment or question not to be personal.

At the same time, the word "accountability" has become popular in a variety of spheres as part of a broader embrace of the language of managerialism in every possible human endeavor. It is a popular way to describe what town hall meetings engender. As an example, alongside a picture of preparations for a town hall meeting, the Town Hall Project tweeted, "This is what account-

---

8. Henry M. Robert III et al., *Robert's Rules of Order, Newly Revised,* 11 ed. (Boston: Da Capo, 2013), 201, 43, 392.

ability looks like."[9] Substituting "accountability" where the word "democracy" usually appears suggests resonance between the two terms; however, they mean different things. "Accountable" means something like "responsible," and it may not be an accident that the word "accountable" adds a fiscal sense to the moral obligations humans owe one another. More generally, though, "to be accountable" means that you are obliged to explain your actions and to face the consequences of your choices. In the most concrete sense, a cashier at a supermarket is accountable when the manager reconciles the goods the cashier rang with the money collected—any shortfall will come out of the cashier's pay.

This notion of accountability has become popular in many political contexts. A February 2018 article about Devin Nunes begins like this: "Apparently, House Intelligence chairman Devin Nunes (R-CA) feels no accountability to his constituents. Not only does he refuse to hold a town hall, the very idea of doing so is ridiculous to him."[10] As the name suggests, Shareblue is a Democratic-leaning media outlet, but the equation of holding town hall meetings and accountability is taken as a given here. The condemnation of elected officials for failing to hold town hall meetings has become commonplace in contemporary politics. Missing from this condemnation, however, is evidence of just how much accountability a town hall meeting can produce. By its nature, a town hall meeting will tend to attract attendees who have some objection to register with the official hosting it. For the sake of argument, we assume the official holds a town

9. Town Hall Project (@townhallproject), "This Is What Accountability Looks Like," Twitter, May 9, 2017, 8:32 p.m., https://twitter.com/townhallproject/status/862102898645381120.

10. Matthew Chapman, "Devin Nunes Melts Down as Hometown Paper Asks if He'll Hold Town Hall," February 22, 2018, Shareblue Media, https://shareblue.com/devin-nunes-fresno-town-hall/.

hall meeting, attendees register their objection, and the town hall meeting concludes. And then what happens? Compared to the cashier with the short drawer, nothing. There is likely some media coverage of the event, especially if the conversation became heated. The elected official returns to his or her duties, and people who attended or followed the conversation can vow to "remember in November," even though that November may be more than five years away. If we pursue the metaphor of the cashier and cash register drawer, it is also possible that a congressperson may feel more accountable in the fiscal sense to his or her donors than to his or her constituents.

As such, these gatherings are what we might call "accountability theater," or an exercise where a politician performs the gestures of accountability without ever having to face actual consequences. For those who attend, town hall meetings can be quite satisfying. As the slogan of Town Hall Project says, these gatherings offer citizens a chance to show up and speak out. Unlike a town meeting, however, the outcomes of this speaking out in town hall meetings are often difficult to discern. Constituent service town halls raise a question: Are the limitations of speaking and hearing as metaphors for the democratic process features or bugs?

Town Hall Meeting as Campus Spectacle

IF THE CONSTITUENT SERVICE town hall meeting allows politicians to perform accountability theater, the town hall meeting has emerged as a way for a university to perform similar work on campus. The campus town hall meeting can present a simulacrum of affective labor by university administration, offering students, faculty, and staff the same kind of cathartic ritual we saw with the constituent service town hall meeting. At the same time, the campus town hall meeting overlaps with the corporate town hall meeting when it functions as a tool of campus governance. Campus town hall meetings can be important outlets for a community when they are held in the wake of an incident that traumatized some portion of the campus community. But this same type of meeting can also take a managerial form that often does more to provoke trauma than to allay it. Especially in times of financial austerity, university officials will hold town hall meetings to announce decisions that university leaders have already made. As with constituent service town halls, the difference between a conversation before a decision and a conversation after a decision is the essence of what separates these rituals from anything like a deliberative democratic process.

As an example of the logic of the managerial campus town hall meeting, consider the following 2014 invitation from Robert H. Jones, the provost of Clemson University, to the faculty and staff: "A strong university is built on the engagement of its faculty, staff and students. For that reason, President Clements and I invite you to our first State of the University town hall, which will take place from 1–2:30 p.m., Wednesday, Nov. 19 at Tillman Hall auditorium. . . . During the event, President Clements will deliver his State of the University address and I will talk about the university's strategic planning process."[1]

This event took place almost exactly a year into President Clements's tenure at Clemson. This email from his provost is symptomatic of the kind of transformation the institution of the town hall meeting can undergo on campus. To begin, this event is a mash-up of two political rituals: the town meeting and the State of the Union address. At the federal level, the State of the Union discharges the president's constitutional obligation to "give to the Congress Information of the State of the Union, and recommend to their Consideration such measures as he shall judge necessary and expedient." In addition, many state and municipal governments have similar events called "State of the State" or "State of the City."

Like the constituent service town hall meeting, the State of the Union address is a prerogative of someone who holds an office rather than an event that determines who will hold an office. As such, a "State of the University town hall" verges into incoherence—the "State of the" part implies a unilateral delivery of information, while the "town hall" part suggests some kind of deliberative process, or at least the appearance of such an exchange. At the same time, the provost's language suggests

1. Robert H. Jones, e-mail to Clemson University Faculty and Staff, November 18, 2014.

that this ritualized form of the town hall meeting has become naturalized: "Because the campus community will be the drivers of our goals and our plan to get there, it is important for us to be transparent in every step of the process. While we are there to share information, it is equally important for us to hear from you. Toward that end, the campus town hall will include a question and answer session."[2] Specifying that a campus town hall includes a question and answer session suggests that there could be a town hall that does not include a question and answer session, which would be something like a staged reading of a press release. But in any case, the primary business of this town hall meeting is to "share information," even as the rhetoric of the email affirms the importance of the campus community.

The language of transparency is also telling here. Transparency is better than its absence in government, but objects either are or are not transparent. So the invocation of transparency suggests that there is an object, either transparent or opaque, interposed between the members of the community and the process that affects them. As Gregory A. Petsko succinctly observed in an open letter to the president of SUNY–Albany about a proposal to eliminate foreign language programs, "You did call a town meeting, but it was to discuss your plan, not to let the university craft its own."[3] The ritualized nature of these events can lurch toward self-parody. For example, a 2018 town hall meeting for Clemson student-athletes solicited prescreened questions for the event and required student-athletes to submit a "comment

2. Jones to Clemson Faculty and Staff.

3. Gregory A. Petsko, "Open Letter to SUNY Albany," November 22, 2010, *Inside Higher Ed*, https://www.insidehighered.com/views/2010/11/22/open-letter-suny-albany.

of appreciation" if they wished to ask a "question of importance" to the athletic director.[4]

Examples of campus town hall events like this could be multiplied endlessly—if you attend or work for a university, there may well be a message inviting you to one in your inbox right now. Unless your university is a radical outlier, managerial town hall meetings like this probably have a similar structure and function of relaying news about decisions leadership has already made rather than gathering to make decisions. At the same time, meetings like this also normalize the town hall meeting as a unilateral managerial process. It might not be overstating the case to suggest that town hall meetings hosted by educational institutions work to lower expectations for the democratic nature of all town hall meetings.

A 2009 town hall meeting at the University of California San Diego (UCSD) demonstrates how the town hall meeting inverts the structure and function of the town meeting. The intrinsic power of a town lies in the power to tax and spend. This power is regulated by the town meeting. The power to tax, and thus to spend, devolves from the state's monopoly on the power to kill, imprison, and confiscate—if you don't pay your taxes, you eventually go to jail. Aspects of this power are distributed variously at the national, state, and town levels, but the degree of autonomy a town can claim is a function of its ability to tax and spend, as well as to deliberate on how much to tax and how much to spend.

In the UCSD instance, the deliberation suggested by a town hall meeting is a ritual. The budgetary decisions have been made elsewhere, and it falls to the UCSD leadership to implement them:

4. Tori Neimann, e-mail to Clemson University Student-Athlete Advisory Council, March 13, 2018.

Salary cuts, furloughs, retirement benefits, equity and the need for political action were on the minds of the more than 2,000 UC San Diego faculty and staff members who turned out in the past two weeks for a series of town hall meetings outlining how the University of California plans to respond to cuts in state funding. During the meetings, Chancellor Marye Anne Fox presented the three options offered by the UC Office of the President, including an 8 percent pay cut, furloughs equating to an 8 percent cut and a mix of pay cuts and furloughs equivalent to an 8 percent decrease in salary. Employees making less than $46,000 a year would take a 4 percent cut. Fox also took questions and feedback from the audience.[5]

Managerial events like these suggest some of the inherent challenges facing a university town hall meeting intended to address a campus in crisis. Regardless of the challenges, such events remain commonplace. In the fall of 2015, the University of Kansas held a town hall meeting as a response to racial tensions on *other* campuses, including the University of Missouri and Yale University. The press release from this event offers a compact summary of the considerations driving the reactive campus town hall meeting:

LAWRENCE—Recent events at Yale University, the University of Missouri and other schools have amplified the ongoing national conversation about race and, more broadly, about respect and responsibility. To further the discussion, the University of Kansas will host a town hall meeting on the topic of race, respect and responsibility at 4 p.m. Wednesday, Nov. 11, in the Big 12 Room of the Kansas Union. The town hall meeting is designed to be an open conversation among students, faculty and staff on the topics of race and inclusion, as well as respect and responsibility. The goal is to create an affirming space for voices from a number of

---

5. Ioana Patringenaru, "Faculty, Staff Have Voices Heard at Chancellor Town Halls on Budget Cuts," *This Week @ UCSD,* June 29, 2009, https://ucsdnews.ucsd.edu/archive/thisweek/2009/06/29_townhall.asp.

communities and backgrounds to be heard and considered. The event is organized by the Office of Student Affairs and the Office of Diversity and Equity, in conjunction with the Office of Multicultural Affairs. "Diversity is a foundational value for the University of Kansas," said Nate Thomas, vice provost for diversity and equity, "and we remain committed to fostering a welcoming and inclusive campus environment where individuals of all backgrounds can succeed and feel comfortable. Additionally, we want our students to be part of the national conversation on race and respect, a conversation that has accelerated in recent weeks on campuses across the country. This town hall meeting is an opportunity for us to advance the conversation."[6]

The language of the press release reveals more of the logic of an event like this than its sponsors might intend. The big news concerning this town hall meeting is that it will be held—in other words, the salient news is that the event even exists, as far as the University of Kansas is concerned. Framing the meeting in this way suggests that it is a foregone conclusion that it will not produce any newsworthy outcomes—the news is that the university cares, and that is that. The only update on this town hall in the University of Kansas press release archives indicates that Chancellor Bernadette Gray-Little would be moderator. It fell to external media sources to report how the town hall unfolded, which turned out to include a protest by African American students.[7] Diagnosing the dynamic often present in events like these, Katherine Rainey, one of the protesting students, an-

6. The University of Kansas "University to Host Town Hall Meeting on Race, Respect, Responsibility," November 9, 2015, https://news.ku.edu/2015/11/09/university-host-town-hall-meeting-race-respect-responsibility.

7. Emily Donovan, "Black Students Interrupt Univ. of Kansas Town Hall in Wake of Missouri Protest," *USA Today*, November 11, 2015, https://web.archive.org/web/20151114012133/http://college.usatoday.com/2015/11/12/black-students-interrupt-univeristy-of-kansas-town-hall/.

nounced to the assembly, "Today's only purpose is to silence and appease students." Responding to these events, the University of Kansas deployed the same rhetoric of seeing and hearing we observed with constituent service town halls.[8]

The University of Kansas was far from alone. As a sample, in October of 2016, the University of Memphis president announced a town hall meeting in response to racist incidents on campus.[9] Just after the 2016 presidential election, Southern Methodist University student leaders held a town hall to address an uptick in racist incidents since the election.[10]

A series of events at American University in the spring of 2017 indicates the appeal of the town hall meeting to administrators, while the student response suggests the limitations of the town hall meeting. Many of the students attending the meeting left early in frustration: "Students said the meeting recapped what people already knew and did not go far enough to address what the university would do. . . . Some administrators went into the crowd to try and assure students they are being heard."[11] Considering that the next academic year at American

8. The University of Kansas, (@KUNews), "Thank you everyone who spoke & attended the #KUconvo tonight. We see you, we hear you; YOU MATTER. Please continue the conversation with us," Twitter, November 11, 2015, 7:23 p.m., https://twitter.com/KUnews/status/664599382315171846.

9. Jeannie Hornish Rakow, "Campus Response to Recent Incidents," The University of Memphis President's Blog, October 3, 2016, https://blogs.memphis.edu/president/2016/10/03/campus-response-to-recent-incidents/.

10. Olivia Nguyen, "SMU Student Leaders Host Town Meeting, Discuss Incidents of Hateful Behavior on Campus," *The Daily Campus*, November 17, 2016, https://www.smudailycampus.com/news/smu-association-of-black-students-host-town-meeting-discuss-incidents-of-hateful-behavior-on-campus.

11. Tom Fitzgerald, "Upset American University Students March Out of Meeting on Campus Hate Crime Incident," Fox 5 DC, May 2, 2017,

University opened with another racist incident, the frustration of these students is understandable. Administrators sought to mollify students of color by telling them they were being heard. Racist incidents continued.[12] The campus town hall offers many opportunities for a university to listen but does very little to compel a university to act.

Westfield State University, on its Bias Incident Response Team (BIRT) webpage, demonstrates how town hall meetings are embedded in the culture of the contemporary U.S. university. In the wake of a bias incident report, which is "any behavior or act . . . which is personally directed against or targeted toward an individual or group . . . based on race, color, religion, sex, sexual orientation, gender identity or expression . . ." there will be both an "individual response" and a "community response." The community responses may include the following:

Provide additional support for those directly affected by the bias incident

Student/campus forum

Campus notices and fact sharing as appropriate (e.g. campus newspaper article, e-mail alerts, text notification, fliers, website updates, etc.)

Educational programming

Response to the media, if appropriate

http://www.fox5dc.com/news/local-news/upset-american-university -students-march-out-of-meeting-on-campus-hate-crime-incident.

12. Shira Stein and Sarah Latimer, "Confederate Flag Posters, with Cotton Attached, Found at American University," *The Washington Post,* September 27, 2017, https://www.washingtonpost.com/news /grade-point/wp/2017/09/27/confederate-flag-posters-with-cotton -attached-found-at-american-university/?noredirect=on&utm _term=.8199615386e5.

Personal counseling for students

Town hall meetings

Speaker rallies

Policy revision recommendations[13]

In some ways Westfield's BIRT webpage is a model for universities in offering a clear outline of the consequences of a bias incident on campus. At the same time, the town hall meeting is as an end in itself in terms of responding to these incidents. It is worth noting that town hall meetings, along with student/campus forum and speaker rallies, come before "policy revision recommendations," and even those are just recommendations.

These meetings can be both an important part of campus life and part of a more transparent model of running a campus. It would be worse for university leaders to implement new strategic plans without indicating what they are. It would be worse for university leaders to ignore traumatic events on campus or around the country that affect their students' well-being. At the same time, the bifurcation of town hall meetings into administrative and affective subcategories effectively segregates the university that speaks (announcing new strategic plans) from the university that listens (fielding student concerns about sexual violence or racist incidents). It is reductive, but perhaps not unfair, to suggest that the burgeoning category of student affairs professionals creates a category of university employees whose job it is to make students feel heard, freeing up other administrators to do the work of actually running the university. At the same time, student affairs professionals are often put in

13. Westfield State University, "Bias Incident Response Team" (accessed January 31, 2019), https://www.westfield.ma.edu/bias-incident-response-team.

the position of simply viewing the college student as a paying customer of tuition and room and board. This conception of student as customer echoes some of the alarming trends Wendy Brown details in her consideration of higher education in the era of neoliberalism, which she calls "Educating Human Capital." For Brown, "Human capital is distinctly not concerned with acquiring the knowledge and experience needed for intelligent democratic citizenship."[14] Instead of engagement in any kind of deliberation with jurisdictional power over the future shape of the university, the campus town hall focuses on making students feel as if they have been heard. The culture of these campus town halls cleaves the deliberative process in two and works to disenfranchise the community that is ostensibly the reason for these meetings in the first place. The campus town hall meeting disrupts the deliberative process, even as it seeks its aura.

One of the peculiarities of the campus town meeting is that it exists outside the contemporary university's infatuation with outcomes. For instructional design, "learning outcomes" have become the coin of the realm. At the instructional level, embracing "learning outcomes" can be an exercise in finding ways to say that wheels are round: "In this class on medieval literature, we will learn about medieval literature by reading medieval literature." But the demand for learning outcomes is also one way to impose a neoliberal rhetoric of college as a place to acquire skills to compete in the twenty-first-century economy on top of a more traditional notion of college as a place to learn things. If education as an end in itself is a fading idea, the campus town hall meeting asserts itself as an end in itself. A campus town hall meeting where leadership announces a strategic plan does exactly just that. The point of the reactive campus town hall meeting

14. Brown, 177.

is simply that it has taken place. As such, it is evidence in and of itself that the university has addressed whatever issue there is.

Beyond an institution's performance of empathy, the campus town meeting's response to an incident can also unfold as Sarah Ahmed describes in *The Cultural Politics of Emotion*. Considering the political work of shame, Ahmed observes, "By witnessing what is shameful about the past, the nation can 'live up to' the ideals that secure its identity or being in the present. The shameful thing interrupts the pride we have in the nation, and the same thing can work at a collegiate valence—this shameful thing that is 'not who we are,' because it is shameful, because we are proud of who we are, as Tigers or Wildcats or Bulldogs, and therefore the shameful thing is aberrant, even if it is routine."[15]

15. Sarah Ahmed, *The Cultural Politics of Emotion,* second edition (New York: Routledge, 2015), 108–9.

Town Hall Meeting as Corporate Event

THE TOWN HALL MEETING FORMAT also offers a way for firms, or their CEOs, to communicate with employees, customers, and vendors. One index of the popularity of corporate town hall meetings is that planning and presenting them has become an industry unto itself. For instance, Davis & Company is a consulting firm focused on helping firms communicate with their own employees. As their website details, "Communicating change to employees can be a challenge, especially if the change has a big impact on their jobs." Specifically, "Leaders and managers have an important role in communicating where the organization is headed and what employees need to do to support it."[1] Evidently one of the ways this firm can help your firm with this task is to host better town halls. The question of what makes a town hall good is one we will return to.

Indeed, corporate town hall meetings have become so ritualistic that in 2017, it was possible for one of the many thought leaders in the industry to propose something akin to the Protestant

1. "Services," Davis & Company (accessed February 7, 2019), https://www.davisandco.com/services.

Reformation—but for town hall culture. According to a blog post from Poll Everywhere, a company that sells software intended to make town hall meetings more interactive, change begins when CEOs "rethink town hall meetings as two-way conversations." On one level, this is blue-sky thinking akin to "wheels, but round," but as the post details, "The town hall meeting—that staple of corporate employee relations—is evolving. Gone are the days of highly-staged annual shows with bright lights and timed musical interludes, topped off with a tightly-vetted CEO Q&A. No more fog machines. No more rock concerts." The absence of fog machines would come as no surprise to a veteran of actual town meetings. But the need to move beyond such flashiness suggests that within corporate town hall culture, spectacle is much more entrenched than democratic process.[2]

There are numerous corporations whose town halls could serve as examples of this culture. Apple Inc.'s engagement with the idea of the town hall meeting is more intense than some but by no means exceptional. Until the recent shift to a larger structure named for Steve Jobs, the principal space for public announcements on the Apple campus was an auditorium called Town Hall. Because Apple restricts pubic access to the entire campus, it functions as a corporate rather than residential gated community. Wendy Brown observes, "While corporations developed research and administrative 'campuses,' universities have become increasingly corporate in physical appearance, financial structure, evaluation, metrics, management style, personnel, advertising and promotion."[3] This union of the university and the

    2. "Rethink Town Hall Meetings as Two-Way Conversations," *Polleverywhere* (blog) (accessed February 7, 2019), https://blog .polleverywhere.com/town-hall-meeting-format/.
    3. Brown, 199.

corporation under the sign of neoliberalism may remind some of the final moments of George Orwell's *Animal Farm*.

On one level, one imagines that calling this structure Town Hall is an effort to humanize a giant tech firm, indeed one that has built its whole brand around humanizing technology. At the same time, the name strikes a false note. A corporation is not a town, and everyone who works for the corporation knows it. Pretending the employees of a corporation are citizens of a town is like when universities pretend that its students, faculty, staff, alumni, and donors constitute a "family." But at least everyone knows that families are not democratic. The evocation of a town as the model for a corporation conflates what it means to be a citizen and what it means to be an employee in disturbing ways.

Even as Apple shifted its base for public announcements from Town Hall to a new, larger underground facility named for Steve Jobs, it doubled down on the town rhetoric. Per a 2017 announcement, Apple's retail outlets, which were previously known as "stores," would be rebranded as "town squares." This announcement was treated with derision, but Apple has moved forward with the first of these flagship stores in Chicago. Privatization in many forms is one of the hallmarks of neoliberalism—indeed, it was Margaret Thatcher's signature move. In the United States, Mike Davis narrated the privatization of public space many years ago. What Davis's *City of Quartz* did not anticipate is that the very concepts of public life, like the public square, could be privatized along with the spaces that supported them. A 2017 report details Apple's plan to rebrand its iPhone showrooms: "Apple Stores will transform from simply commercial spaces to locations where the company will develop 'communities': host concerts, lead workshops, offer up meeting rooms, and teach everything from coding to photography to music-making. Apple frames these disciplines as modern equivalents to the medieval *trivium*—an essential educational resource that makes a person a person."[4] As Alexis Madrigal observed, "In adopting the faux democratic language of Facebook and Twitter, Apple has made the perfect physical metaphor for the largely ineffable problem the internet poses to democracy."[5]

If Apple deploys town hall rhetoric to woo customers, another much iconic consumer brand uses it to manage times of change and uncertainty. In the wake of Amazon's acquisition of Whole Foods Market, Whole Foods's CEO held a town hall for employees. Interspersed with notions of citizenship implied by a town hall, John Mackey leaned on the trope of family to describe this new "corporation": "And we want Whole Foods people to be at Amazon. . . . When this deal closes, we're all Amazon people. We're not Whole Foods people and Amazon people. We're all Amazon people. We're one large tribe, one large family."[6] In light of Mackey's account of this deal as a courtship and marriage, this language is not surprising but also possibly not entirely reassuring for his audience.

Lower profile companies also embrace the culture of the town hall meeting. In an article hailing a Rochester, New York, data protection company as the best midsized employer in the region, the *Democrat and Chronicle* hailed the founder and CEO's commitment to town hall meetings. An employee quoted in the

4. James Vincent, "Apple Calling Its Stores 'Town Squares' Is a Pretentious Farce," *The Verge,* September 12, 2017, https://www.theverge.com/2017/9/12/16296460/apple-self-love-iphonex-iphone8-event.

5. Alexis C. Madrigal, "The Great Thing about Apple Christening Their Stores 'Town Squares,'" *The Atlantic,* September 13, 2017, https://www.theatlantic.com/technology/archive/2017/09/the-great-thing-about-apple-christening-their-stores-town-squares/539667/.

6. "8 Interesting Tidbits from Whole Foods's Town Hall Following the Amazon Acquisition," *Entrepreneur,* June 20, 2017, https://www.entrepreneur.com/article/296101.

article "noted the monthly town hall meetings, hosted by founder and CEO Austin McChord, to share the latest news on what and how the organization is doing." As the employee explains, our founder and CEO "is so incredibly transparent. . . . He'll tell us anything and everything about the company and trusts us with the information. That trickles down and makes me feel like I can be transparent with my team."[7] The language here shades toward the popular corporate notion of "best practices," or ways of doing things that are applicable to almost any business endeavor. As Wendy Brown points out, "Best practices bring with them the ends and values with which they are imbricated; by the experts' own accounts, these are market values."[8]

Ironically, advice about town hall meeting best practices can project the culture of the town hall meeting back on to actual town meetings. For example, Convene, a company that hosts corporate events, describes town hall meeting dos and don'ts:

> Town hall meetings have served as a means of public communication between groups since the early colonial era in New England. Traditionally, these town halls were a public meeting or event conducted to open dialogue between town officials and citizens. In the modern workplace, corporate town halls parallel that tradition, opening up the lines of communication between executives and employees.[9]

This hierarchy of "executives and employees" is inimical to the

7. Krista Gleason, "Top Midsize Employer: Datto Thrives by Inspiring Its People to Do Well," *Rochester Democrat & Chronicle,* March 28, 2018, https://www.democratandchronicle.com/story/money /business/2018/03/29/datto-austin-mcchord-rochester-top -workplaces-midsize-employer/323753002/.

8. Brown, *Undoing The Demos,* 138.

9. Andrea Duke, "5 Dos and Don'ts for Planning a Corporate Town Hall," *Catalyst* (blog), Convene (Accessed February 7, 2019), https:// convene.com/catalyst/5-dos-donts-planning-corporate-town-hall/.

democratic structure of a town meeting, but it's easy to imagine this distorted corporate form taking root as *the* popular understanding of how town meetings work. According to this account, once there were town officials and citizens, and now there are executives and employees. Again, we see citizenship reimagined through the fiscal prism of either employee or customer. At the same time, this analogy elides a key distinction between the leadership of a small New England town and a modern corporation. While town officials are citizens, remain citizens while holding office, and will still be citizens when their terms are up, the distinction between "executive" and "employee" is much more permanent. As offhand as it is, the lede to this article suggests that we have a diminishing ability to recognize what is and is not democracy.

The Future of the Town Hall Meeting

IF THE TOWN HALL MEETING campaign stop is the first significant step away from the original town meeting, a corporate town
hall meeting with a political agenda might be the biggest depar-
ture yet. However, at their 2018 Donor Summit, the Koch brothers outlined a midterm election strategy that included town halls.
This is a staple of the Koch playbook—during the 2017 debate on
tax reform, the Koch brothers held more than one hundred town
halls and announced plans for more during the 2018 election
cycle.[1] One of the most notable recent town halls suggests what
the future of the town hall might be. On February 21, 2018, CNN
hosted a televised town hall on the recent horrific mass shooting
at Marjory Stoneman Douglas High School in Parkland, Florida.[2]

---

1. Ylan Mui, "Conservative Koch Brothers' Network to Spend up to
$400 Million for the Midterm Election Cycle—Including $20 million to
Sell the GOP Tax Law," *Politics,* CNBC, January 28, 2018, https://www
.cnbc.com/2018/01/27/koch-brothers-network-to-spend-400-million
-in-midterm-election-cycle.html.

2. "CNN Announces Town Hall with Students, Parents Affected by
Florida School Shooting," *Politics,* CNN, February 19, 2018, https://www
.cnn.com/2018/02/17/politics/parkland-town-hall/index.html.

The live event, held at BB&T Center, included classmates of the victims, parents, and members of the community. CNN also invited prominent Florida lawmakers and politicians, as well as President Trump, to take part in the town hall.

This particular school shooting has motivated the survivors to advocate for change, and I hope that this impetus can sustain a different and better approach for the safety of students. At the same time, the town hall meeting's evolution continues to reshape the paradigm of what it is and does. Most notably, one of the most prominent aspects of the Florida town hall meeting was the absence of elected officials. In particular, Florida Governor Rick Scott faced criticism from survivors of the shooting for not accepting CNN's invitation to participate.[3]

The anger of student-activists like Sarah Chadwick is easy to understand. It also emerges in a context that is worth considering. To start, there was a horrific event, all the more horrific because of how routine school shootings have become in the United States. In the context of this discussion of town hall meetings, the particular evolution of this Florida town hall meeting warrants some thought. We have a TV network that convened a public gathering to discuss a topic of national interest. As the host, CNN invited politicians, survivors, and other interested parties, including NRA spokesperson, Dana Loesch. CNN's role here was complex—the network's act of convening this town hall meeting was itself a news story that CNN then disseminated. Politicians who chose to attend or not attend generated another news story. If this event changed the relationship between politicians and

---

3. Sarah Chadwick (@Sarahchadwickk), "Upset to hear our governor Rick Scott wont be attending the town hall meeting on Wednesday. To be fair, he does have an A+ rating from the NRA, and i think he's scared of my peers and I," Twitter, February 22, 2018, 12:56 a.m., https://twitter.com/Sarahchadwickk/status/965827435567730688.

pro-gun lobbyists, we can hope that this change will make the United States a safer place. At the same time, it is striking how the roles of various parties have evolved from the town meeting paradigm. Rather than a municipality, a TV network was the host of this event. It was an event that people were or were not invited to. It took place in the BB&T Arena, which is usually the home of the NHL's Florida Panthers. This town hall was an event for media, not a structure of governance.

If there is a rough taxonomy of political, academic, and corporate town hall meetings that descend from the original town meeting, this CNN meeting blended the three. It was political in that it served as a form of constituent service; it had the trauma management function of some academic town halls; and it was hosted, organized, and sponsored by a corporate entity. As such, this gathering straddled usual conceptions of public and private. Because elected officials were present, they were, to some extent, accountable to their constituents. At the same time, this was a private and not public event since CNN was in charge of the guest list. An invitation-only gathering cannot, by definition, be fully inclusive, but there is a difference between people not invited who did not come and officials who were invited but chose not to attend, such as Florida Governor Rick Scott. For the officials brave enough to show up, it may have felt like attending a demonstration to get their fair share of abuse. But whatever benefits the event offered survivors, parents, and other citizens, this process also functioned as a spectacle that benefited CNN by attracting viewers. As Todd Starnes of Fox News commented, "It's a public flogging, not a town hall meeting. Hope the ratings are worth it, @jaketapper and @CNN."[4]

4. Todd Starnes, (@toddstarnes), "It's a public flogging, not a town hall meeting. Hope the ratings are worth it, @jaketapper and @CNN), Twitter, February, 21, 2018, 10:03 p.m., https://twitter.com/toddstarnes /status/966508702340734978.

Starnes might have overstated the case, but the Parkland town hall meeting on CNN felt more like a pep rally for gun control than a democratic, deliberative process a town meeting should be. This concept of town hall meeting as pep rally is also one that Starnes's own network has employed. In January of 2019, Fox News presented the "Battle at the Border Town Hall," which focused on immigration and border security and was hosted by Brian Kilmeade and Tomi Lahren.[5] This spectacle—with a name worthy of a heavyweight boxing match—took the town hall as pep rally one step further, as chants of "Build that Wall" periodically erupted from the audience.

5. Joe Concha, "Fox News to Host 'Battle at the Border' Town Hall Featuring Kilmeade, Lahren, *The Hill,* January 24, 2019, https://thehill.com/homenews/media/426811-fox-news-to-host-battle-at-the-border-town-hall-featuring-kilmeade-lahren.

Conclusion

FOR BOTH CNN AND FOX NEWS, the town hall format offers a spectacle designed to advance a particular political agenda and to boost the networks' ratings. Both of these town halls also offer simulated deliberation to an audience watching at home. "Town hall" imbues these events, and other such events will follow with their cozy aura of democracy, even as they represent a total abrogation of the democratic ideals of the town meeting. In writing what amounts to a critique of the evolution of the town meeting, I hope that I do not put myself among those writers who revere the New England town meeting as a sort of democratic Camelot we cannot hope to regain in these sad, latter days. At the same time, I think that paying attention to what town meetings and town hall meetings are and do is worth the effort for people who support democracy as a system of government. To summarize its ongoing metamorphosis, the original town meeting is when people gather to vote on the future shape of their institution. In the town hall meeting as political debate, political event, or academic town hall, the people gather so the institution's representatives can listen. In the town hall meeting as corporate event, the people gather so the institution can announce something, perform a ritual of listening to its constituents, or broadcast this ritual to audiences watching on television.

The town hall meeting used in response to trauma or grievances—in other words, town hall meeting as press conference—is perhaps harder to pin down than the original town meeting. But its transitional role might warrant further consideration from scholars of trauma and of public culture. For one thing, it is worth considering just what it means for a politician or the representative of a university to listen. Listening exists as a more active variant of the passive state of hearing, but listening also imposes no obligation. In contemporary language, listening is perhaps an easier way to say empathizing, but even empathizing does not carry the promise of any action on behalf of the speaker. The shift from deliberation to listening as the function of a town hall meeting is the more straightforward part of this equation. The abstraction inherent in democracy—including the fact there will always be a minority who does not get what they want—means that making appeals and airing grievances will not always elicit the action one hopes for. (Indeed, in the Trump era, much of current "resistance" activity consists of a quixotic proliferation of appeals that are delivered with the full knowledge they will be ignored.) So, to some extent, being on the losing side of a tax increase vote at the town level conditions citizens to politely smile and nod, just as they do when their senator answers their questions at a town hall meeting.

The shift from listening to announcing is complex but strategic, and the categories overlap. For instance, a racist incident on campus will traumatize some members of that community, and the university's leadership might well hold a town hall to provide space for members of the community to talk and for the university to listen. At the same time, if a university announces a new austerity plan that will traumatize some members of the community, the university might well hold a town hall to enact the announcement of those austerity measures, even as it performs the act of listening to objections to this plan. What works for the university works for the corporation—at the end of a town hall meeting to announce corporate restructuring that will cost jobs, there is nothing for employees to vote on.

If this brief study has a conclusion beyond surveying the various ways that individuals and institutions have co-opted a basic form of democracy, I hope that it reemphasizes that without voting, there is no democracy. This is not a sophisticated political analysis, but it is worth bearing in mind, especially in an age of widespread gerrymandering and voter suppression. For citizens who are unhappy with the status quo, it would be a disaster to confuse being heard at a town hall meeting with being heard at a ballot box.

Acknowledgments

Thanks Aaron, Abby, Alex, Aleesa, Amanda, Angela, Audrey, Babes, Barnard, Ben, Bill, Birma, Brigitte, Buddy, Buster, Caitlin, Carol, Charles, Dani, Deb, Daniel, Dante, Dave, Davey, Dinah, Doug, Edythe, Elizabeth, Erin, Eva, Fable, Fischer, Holly, Jennifer, Jim, James, Jason, Jasper, Jeff, Jen, John, Johnna, Jon, Jonathan, Jillian, Julia, Julian, Katie, Keith, Keri, Laura, Lee, Leslie, Lisa, Lulu, Margs, Margo, Mary, Maryanne, Maura, Mark, Max, Meels, Meredith, Michael, Mike, Neil, Nicholas, Nick's, Oliver, Pat, Penny, Pete, Polar, Raymond, Ren, Renee Rhea, Rich, Rick, Rosemary, Ruby, Ryan, Sam, Sandra, Sarah, Seren, Seth, Shenice, Spencer, Steve, Susanna, Susie, Suzanne, Teo, Thomas, Tom, Townes, Walt, Walter, & Winnie, but mostly, Amy.

(Continued from page iii)

Shannon Mattern
Deep Mapping the Media City

Steven Shaviro
No Speed Limit: Three Essays on Accelerationism

Jussi Parikka
The Anthrobscene

Reinhold Martin
Mediators: Aesthetics, Politics, and the City

John Hartigan Jr.
Aesop's Anthropology: A Multispecies Approach

Jonathan Beecher Field is associate professor of English at Clemson University and author of *Errands into the Metropolis: New England Dissidents in Revolutionary London.*